# Daily Wellness Journal



NAME

ADDRESS

E-MAIL ADDRESS

WEBSITE

PHONE                                    FAX

EMERGENCY CONTACT PERSON

PHONE                                    FAX

# Date _______________ Weight _______________

## WAKE UP

## BED TIME

## SLEEP (HRS)

## I'M GRATEFUL FOR

## ACTIVITIES

## EXERCISE LOG

## MOOD TRACKER

- ☐ MORNING
- ☐ AFTERNOON
- ☐ NIGHT

WATER INTAKE

## WHAT I ATE TODAY

**BREAKFAST** ...........................................................................

**LUNCH** ...........................................................................

**DINNER** ...........................................................................

**SNACK** ...........................................................................

## NOTES

Happiness Rating ⭐ ⭐ ⭐ ⭐ ⭐

# Date _______________ Weight _______________

## WAKE UP

## BED TIME

## SLEEP (HRS)

## I'M GRATEFUL FOR

## ACTIVITIES

## EXERCISE LOG

## MOOD TRACKER

- ☐ MORNING
- ☐ AFTERNOON
- ☐ NIGHT

**WATER INTAKE**

## WHAT I ATE TODAY

**BREAKFAST** ...........................................................................

**LUNCH** ...........................................................................

**DINNER** ...........................................................................

**SNACK** ...........................................................................

## NOTES

Happiness Rating  ☆ ☆ ☆ ☆ ☆

# Date _______________    Weight _______________

## WAKE UP

## BED TIME

## SLEEP (HRS)

## I'M GRATEFUL FOR

## ACTIVITIES

## EXERCISE LOG

## MOOD TRACKER

- ☐ MORNING
- ☐ AFTERNOON
- ☐ NIGHT

WATER INTAKE

## WHAT I ATE TODAY

BREAKFAST ............................................................................

LUNCH ............................................................................

DINNER ............................................................................

SNACK ............................................................................

## NOTES

## Happiness Rating ⭐ ⭐ ⭐ ⭐ ⭐

# Date ............... Weight ...............

## WAKE UP

## BED TIME

## SLEEP (HRS)

## I'M GRATEFUL FOR

..................................................
..................................................
..................................................
..................................................
..................................................
..................................................
..................................................
..................................................

## ACTIVITIES

## EXERCISE LOG

## MOOD TRACKER

☐ MORNING

☐ AFTERNOON

☐ NIGHT

**WATER INTAKE**

## WHAT I ATE TODAY

BREAKFAST ..................................................
LUNCH ..................................................
DINNER ..................................................
SNACK ..................................................

## NOTES

..................................................
..................................................
..................................................
..................................................
..................................................
..................................................

*Happiness Rating* ☆ ☆ ☆ ☆ ☆

# Date _____________   Weight _____________

## WAKE UP

## BED TIME

## SLEEP (HRS)

## I'M GRATEFUL FOR

## ACTIVITIES

## EXERCISE LOG

## MOOD TRACKER

- ☐ MORNING
- ☐ AFTERNOON
- ☐ NIGHT

**WATER INTAKE**

## WHAT I ATE TODAY

**BREAKFAST** ..............................................................................................

**LUNCH** ..............................................................................................

**DINNER** ..............................................................................................

**SNACK** ..............................................................................................

## NOTES

*Happiness Rating* ★ ★ ★ ★ ★

# Date _____________ Weight _____________

## WAKE UP

## BED TIME

## SLEEP (HRS)

## I'M GRATEFUL FOR

## ACTIVITIES

## EXERCISE LOG

## MOOD TRACKER

- ☐ MORNING
- ☐ AFTERNOON
- ☐ NIGHT

**WATER INTAKE**

## WHAT I ATE TODAY

**BREAKFAST** _____________
**LUNCH** _____________
**DINNER** _____________
**SNACK** _____________

## NOTES

*Happiness Rating* ★ ★ ★ ★ ★

# Date _______________ Weight _______________

## WAKE UP

## BED TIME

## SLEEP (HRS)

## I'M GRATEFUL FOR

## ACTIVITIES

## EXERCISE LOG

## MOOD TRACKER

- ☐ MORNING
- ☐ AFTERNOON
- ☐ NIGHT

**WATER INTAKE**

## WHAT I ATE TODAY

**BREAKFAST** ...........................................................................

**LUNCH** ...........................................................................

**DINNER** ...........................................................................

**SNACK** ...........................................................................

## NOTES

*Happiness Rating*  ★ ★ ★ ★ ★

# Date _______________   Weight _______________

## WAKE UP

## BED TIME

## SLEEP (HRS)

## I'M GRATEFUL FOR

## ACTIVITIES

## EXERCISE LOG

## MOOD TRACKER

- ☐ MORNING
- ☐ AFTERNOON
- ☐ NIGHT

**WATER INTAKE**

## WHAT I ATE TODAY

**BREAKFAST** ...................................................................

**LUNCH** ...................................................................

**DINNER** ...................................................................

**SNACK** ...................................................................

## NOTES

Happiness Rating  ☆ ☆ ☆ ☆ ☆

# Date _______________    Weight _______________

## WAKE UP

## BED TIME

## SLEEP (HRS)

## I'M GRATEFUL FOR

## ACTIVITIES

## EXERCISE LOG

## MOOD TRACKER

- ☐ MORNING
- ☐ AFTERNOON
- ☐ NIGHT

**WATER INTAKE**

## WHAT I ATE TODAY

**BREAKFAST** .................................................................

**LUNCH** .................................................................

**DINNER** .................................................................

**SNACK** .................................................................

## NOTES

# Happiness Rating ⭐ ⭐ ⭐ ⭐ ⭐

# Date _____________  Weight _____________

## WAKE UP

## I'M GRATEFUL FOR

..............................................
..............................................
..............................................
..............................................
..............................................
..............................................
..............................................
..............................................

## BED TIME

## SLEEP (HRS)

## ACTIVITIES

## EXERCISE LOG

## MOOD TRACKER

☐ **MORNING**

☐ **AFTERNOON**

☐ **NIGHT**

**WATER INTAKE**

## WHAT I ATE TODAY

**BREAKFAST** ..............................................

**LUNCH** ..............................................

**DINNER** ..............................................

**SNACK** ..............................................

## NOTES

..............................................
..............................................
..............................................
..............................................
..............................................

**Happiness Rating** ⭐ ⭐ ⭐ ⭐ ⭐

Date _______________    Weight _______________

## WAKE UP

## BED TIME

## SLEEP (HRS)

## I'M GRATEFUL FOR

## ACTIVITIES

## EXERCISE LOG

## MOOD TRACKER

- ☐ MORNING
- ☐ AFTERNOON
- ☐ NIGHT

WATER INTAKE

## WHAT I ATE TODAY

**BREAKFAST** .......................................................
**LUNCH** .......................................................
**DINNER** .......................................................
**SNACK** .......................................................

## NOTES

Happiness Rating  ☆ ☆ ☆ ☆ ☆

# Date _______ Weight _______

## WAKE UP

## BED TIME

## SLEEP (HRS)

## I'M GRATEFUL FOR

## ACTIVITIES

## EXERCISE LOG

## MOOD TRACKER

- ☐ MORNING
- ☐ AFTERNOON
- ☐ NIGHT

## WATER INTAKE

## WHAT I ATE TODAY

**BREAKFAST** .................................................................

**LUNCH** .................................................................

**DINNER** .................................................................

**SNACK** .................................................................

## NOTES

*Happiness Rating* ☆ ☆ ☆ ☆ ☆

# Date .................... Weight ....................

## WAKE UP

## BED TIME

## SLEEP (HRS)

## I'M GRATEFUL FOR

## ACTIVITIES

## EXERCISE LOG

## MOOD TRACKER

☐ MORNING

☐ AFTERNOON

☐ NIGHT

**WATER INTAKE**

## WHAT I ATE TODAY

**BREAKFAST** ....................................................

**LUNCH** ....................................................

**DINNER** ....................................................

**SNACK** ....................................................

## NOTES

## Happiness Rating ★ ★ ★ ★ ★

# Date _____________ Weight _____________

## WAKE UP

## BED TIME

## SLEEP (HRS)

## I'M GRATEFUL FOR

## ACTIVITIES

## EXERCISE LOG

## MOOD TRACKER

- ☐ MORNING
- ☐ AFTERNOON
- ☐ NIGHT

**WATER INTAKE**

## WHAT I ATE TODAY

**BREAKFAST** ....................................................

**LUNCH** ....................................................

**DINNER** ....................................................

**SNACK** ....................................................

## NOTES

*Happiness Rating* ☆ ☆ ☆ ☆ ☆

# Date _______ Weight _______

## WAKE UP

## BED TIME

## SLEEP (HRS)

## I'M GRATEFUL FOR

## ACTIVITIES

## EXERCISE LOG

## MOOD TRACKER

- ☐ MORNING
- ☐ AFTERNOON
- ☐ NIGHT

**WATER INTAKE**

## WHAT I ATE TODAY

**BREAKFAST** ..............................................

**LUNCH** ..............................................

**DINNER** ..............................................

**SNACK** ..............................................

## NOTES

*Happiness Rating* ☆ ☆ ☆ ☆ ☆

# Date .................... Weight ....................

## WAKE UP

## BED TIME

## SLEEP (HRS)

## I'M GRATEFUL FOR

.................................................
.................................................
.................................................
.................................................
.................................................
.................................................
.................................................
.................................................

## ACTIVITIES

## EXERCISE LOG

## MOOD TRACKER

- ☐ MORNING
- ☐ AFTERNOON
- ☐ NIGHT

**WATER INTAKE**

## WHAT I ATE TODAY

BREAKFAST ....................................................

LUNCH ....................................................

DINNER ....................................................

SNACK ....................................................

## NOTES

.................................................
.................................................
.................................................
.................................................
.................................................
.................................................

*Happiness Rating* ★ ★ ★ ★ ★

# Date ............... Weight ...............

## WAKE UP

## BED TIME

## SLEEP (HRS)

## I'M GRATEFUL FOR

## ACTIVITIES

## EXERCISE LOG

## MOOD TRACKER

☐ MORNING

☐ AFTERNOON

☐ NIGHT

**WATER INTAKE**

## WHAT I ATE TODAY

**BREAKFAST** ...............................................................................

**LUNCH** ...............................................................................

**DINNER** ...............................................................................

**SNACK** ...............................................................................

## NOTES

Happiness Rating ⭐ ⭐ ⭐ ⭐ ⭐

# Date ............ Weight ............

## WAKE UP

## BED TIME

## SLEEP (HRS)

## I'M GRATEFUL FOR

.......................................................
.......................................................
.......................................................
.......................................................
.......................................................
.......................................................
.......................................................
.......................................................

## ACTIVITIES

## EXERCISE LOG

## MOOD TRACKER

- ☐ MORNING
- ☐ AFTERNOON
- ☐ NIGHT

**WATER INTAKE**

## WHAT I ATE TODAY

**BREAKFAST** ............................................

**LUNCH** ............................................

**DINNER** ............................................

**SNACK** ............................................

## NOTES

.......................................................
.......................................................
.......................................................
.......................................................
.......................................................
.......................................................

*Happiness Rating* ☆ ☆ ☆ ☆ ☆

# Date .............. Weight ..............

## WAKE UP

## BED TIME

## SLEEP (HRS)

## I'M GRATEFUL FOR

## ACTIVITIES

## EXERCISE LOG

## MOOD TRACKER

- ☐ MORNING
- ☐ AFTERNOON
- ☐ NIGHT

**WATER INTAKE**

## WHAT I ATE TODAY

**BREAKFAST** ..............
**LUNCH** ..............
**DINNER** ..............
**SNACK** ..............

## NOTES

*Happiness Rating* ☆ ☆ ☆ ☆ ☆

# Date _______________ Weight _______________

## WAKE UP

## BED TIME

## SLEEP (HRS)

## I'M GRATEFUL FOR

## ACTIVITIES

## EXERCISE LOG

## MOOD TRACKER

- ☐ MORNING
- ☐ AFTERNOON
- ☐ NIGHT

WATER INTAKE

## WHAT I ATE TODAY

**BREAKFAST** ...............................................................

**LUNCH** ...............................................................

**DINNER** ...............................................................

**SNACK** ...............................................................

## NOTES

*Happiness Rating* ☆ ☆ ☆ ☆ ☆

# Date _______________  Weight _______________

## WAKE UP

## BED TIME

## SLEEP (HRS)

## I'M GRATEFUL FOR

## ACTIVITIES

## EXERCISE LOG

## MOOD TRACKER

- ☐ MORNING
- ☐ AFTERNOON
- ☐ NIGHT

**WATER INTAKE**

## WHAT I ATE TODAY

**BREAKFAST** _______________
**LUNCH** _______________
**DINNER** _______________
**SNACK** _______________

## NOTES

Happiness Rating ⭐ ⭐ ⭐ ⭐ ⭐

# Date .............. Weight ..............

## WAKE UP

## BED TIME

## SLEEP (HRS)

## I'M GRATEFUL FOR

## ACTIVITIES

## EXERCISE LOG

## MOOD TRACKER

☐ MORNING

☐ AFTERNOON

☐ NIGHT

WATER INTAKE

## WHAT I ATE TODAY

BREAKFAST .......................

LUNCH .......................

DINNER .......................

SNACK .......................

## NOTES

Happiness Rating ⭐ ⭐ ⭐ ⭐ ⭐

# Date _______________  Weight _______________

## WAKE UP

## BED TIME

## SLEEP (HRS)

## I'M GRATEFUL FOR

## ACTIVITIES

## EXERCISE LOG

## MOOD TRACKER

- ☐ MORNING
- ☐ AFTERNOON
- ☐ NIGHT

**WATER INTAKE**

## WHAT I ATE TODAY

**BREAKFAST** ...................................................

**LUNCH** ...................................................

**DINNER** ...................................................

**SNACK** ...................................................

## NOTES

*Happiness Rating*  ☆ ☆ ☆ ☆ ☆

# Date ............... Weight ...............

## WAKE UP

## BED TIME

## SLEEP (HRS)

## I'M GRATEFUL FOR

....................................................
....................................................
....................................................
....................................................
....................................................
....................................................
....................................................
....................................................

## ACTIVITIES

## EXERCISE LOG

## MOOD TRACKER

- ☐ MORNING
- ☐ AFTERNOON
- ☐ NIGHT

**WATER INTAKE**

## WHAT I ATE TODAY

**BREAKFAST** .................................................
**LUNCH** .................................................
**DINNER** .................................................
**SNACK** .................................................

## NOTES

....................................................
....................................................
....................................................
....................................................
....................................................

## Happiness Rating ☆ ☆ ☆ ☆ ☆

# Date .................. Weight ..................

## WAKE UP

## BED TIME

## SLEEP (HRS)

## I'M GRATEFUL FOR

## ACTIVITIES

## EXERCISE LOG

## MOOD TRACKER

- ☐ MORNING
- ☐ AFTERNOON
- ☐ NIGHT

**WATER INTAKE**

## WHAT I ATE TODAY

**BREAKFAST** ..................................................

**LUNCH** ..................................................

**DINNER** ..................................................

**SNACK** ..................................................

## NOTES

*Happiness Rating* ★ ★ ★ ★ ★

# Date _____________  Weight _____________

## WAKE UP

## BED TIME

## SLEEP (HRS)

## I'M GRATEFUL FOR

## ACTIVITIES

## EXERCISE LOG

## MOOD TRACKER

- ☐ MORNING
- ☐ AFTERNOON
- ☐ NIGHT

**WATER INTAKE**

## WHAT I ATE TODAY

**BREAKFAST** ...........................................................................

**LUNCH** ...........................................................................

**DINNER** ...........................................................................

**SNACK** ...........................................................................

## NOTES

*Happiness Rating* ⭐ ⭐ ⭐ ⭐ ⭐

# Date _______________ Weight _______________

## WAKE UP

## BED TIME

## SLEEP (HRS)

## I'M GRATEFUL FOR

## ACTIVITIES

## EXERCISE LOG

## MOOD TRACKER

- ☐ MORNING
- ☐ AFTERNOON
- ☐ NIGHT

WATER INTAKE

## WHAT I ATE TODAY

**BREAKFAST** _______________________________________

**LUNCH** _______________________________________

**DINNER** _______________________________________

**SNACK** _______________________________________

## NOTES

*Happiness Rating* ☆ ☆ ☆ ☆ ☆

# Date ............... Weight ...............

## WAKE UP

## BED TIME

## SLEEP (HRS)

## I'M GRATEFUL FOR

## ACTIVITIES

## EXERCISE LOG

## MOOD TRACKER

- ☐ MORNING
- ☐ AFTERNOON
- ☐ NIGHT

**WATER INTAKE**

## WHAT I ATE TODAY

BREAKFAST ...............................................................

LUNCH ...............................................................

DINNER ...............................................................

SNACK ...............................................................

## NOTES

*Happiness Rating* ★ ★ ★ ★ ★

# Date ............... Weight ...............

## WAKE UP

## BED TIME

## SLEEP (HRS)

## I'M GRATEFUL FOR

.................................................................................
.................................................................................
.................................................................................
.................................................................................
.................................................................................
.................................................................................
.................................................................................
.................................................................................

## ACTIVITIES

## EXERCISE LOG

## MOOD TRACKER

- ☐ MORNING
- ☐ AFTERNOON
- ☐ NIGHT

**WATER INTAKE**

## WHAT I ATE TODAY

**BREAKFAST** ..................................................................................
**LUNCH** ..................................................................................
**DINNER** ..................................................................................
**SNACK** ..................................................................................

## NOTES

.................................................................................
.................................................................................
.................................................................................
.................................................................................
.................................................................................

# Happiness Rating ☆ ☆ ☆ ☆ ☆

# Date _____________ Weight _____________

## WAKE UP

## BED TIME

## SLEEP (HRS)

## I'M GRATEFUL FOR

## ACTIVITIES

## EXERCISE LOG

## MOOD TRACKER

- ☐ MORNING
- ☐ AFTERNOON
- ☐ NIGHT

**WATER INTAKE**

## WHAT I ATE TODAY

BREAKFAST .................................................................

LUNCH .................................................................

DINNER .................................................................

SNACK .................................................................

## NOTES

Happiness Rating ⭐ ⭐ ⭐ ⭐ ⭐

$Date$ .................... $Weight$ ....................

## WAKE UP

## BED TIME

## SLEEP (HRS)

## I'M GRATEFUL FOR

........................................................
........................................................
........................................................
........................................................
........................................................
........................................................
........................................................

## ACTIVITIES

## EXERCISE LOG

## MOOD TRACKER

☐ MORNING

☐ AFTERNOON

☐ NIGHT

**WATER INTAKE**

## WHAT I ATE TODAY

**BREAKFAST** ........................................................

**LUNCH** ........................................................

**DINNER** ........................................................

**SNACK** ........................................................

## NOTES

........................................................
........................................................
........................................................
........................................................
........................................................
........................................................

$Happiness\ Rating$ ★ ★ ★ ★ ★

# Date _______________ Weight _______________

## WAKE UP

## BED TIME

## SLEEP (HRS)

## I'M GRATEFUL FOR

## ACTIVITIES

## EXERCISE LOG

## MOOD TRACKER

- ☐ MORNING
- ☐ AFTERNOON
- ☐ NIGHT

**WATER INTAKE**

## WHAT I ATE TODAY

**BREAKFAST** ...............................................................

**LUNCH** ...............................................................

**DINNER** ...............................................................

**SNACK** ...............................................................

## NOTES

*Happiness Rating* ☆ ☆ ☆ ☆ ☆

# Date _______ Weight _______

## WAKE UP

## BED TIME

## SLEEP (HRS)

## I'M GRATEFUL FOR

## ACTIVITIES

## EXERCISE LOG

## MOOD TRACKER

- ☐ MORNING
- ☐ AFTERNOON
- ☑ NIGHT

**WATER INTAKE**

## WHAT I ATE TODAY

**BREAKFAST** ...........................................................

**LUNCH** ...........................................................

**DINNER** ...........................................................

**SNACK** ...........................................................

## NOTES

*Happiness Rating* ⭐ ⭐ ⭐ ⭐ ⭐

# Date ......................  Weight ......................

## WAKE UP

## BED TIME

## SLEEP (HRS)

## I'M GRATEFUL FOR

...........................................................
...........................................................
...........................................................
...........................................................
...........................................................
...........................................................
...........................................................
...........................................................

## ACTIVITIES

## EXERCISE LOG

## MOOD TRACKER

- ☐ MORNING
- ☐ AFTERNOON
- ☐ NIGHT

**WATER INTAKE**

## WHAT I ATE TODAY

**BREAKFAST** ...........................................................
**LUNCH** ...........................................................
**DINNER** ...........................................................
**SNACK** ...........................................................

## NOTES

...........................................................
...........................................................
...........................................................
...........................................................
...........................................................

*Happiness Rating*  ☆ ☆ ☆ ☆ ☆

Date ............... Weight ...................

## WAKE UP

## BED TIME

## SLEEP (HRS)

## I'M GRATEFUL FOR

..................................................
..................................................
..................................................
..................................................
..................................................
..................................................
..................................................
..................................................

## ACTIVITIES

## EXERCISE LOG

## MOOD TRACKER

☐ MORNING
☐ AFTERNOON
☐ NIGHT

WATER INTAKE

## WHAT I ATE TODAY

**BREAKFAST** ....................................................
**LUNCH** ....................................................
**DINNER** ....................................................
**SNACK** ....................................................

## NOTES

..................................................
..................................................
..................................................
..................................................
..................................................

Happiness Rating ⭐ ⭐ ⭐ ⭐ ⭐

# Date ........................  Weight ........................

## WAKE UP

## BED TIME

## SLEEP (HRS)

## I'M GRATEFUL FOR

....................................................
....................................................
....................................................
....................................................
....................................................
....................................................
....................................................
....................................................

## ACTIVITIES

## EXERCISE LOG

## MOOD TRACKER

- ☐ MORNING
- ☐ AFTERNOON
- ☐ NIGHT

**WATER INTAKE**

## WHAT I ATE TODAY

**BREAKFAST** ....................................................
**LUNCH** ....................................................
**DINNER** ....................................................
**SNACK** ....................................................

## NOTES

....................................................
....................................................
....................................................
....................................................
....................................................
....................................................

## Happiness Rating  ☆ ☆ ☆ ☆ ☆

# Date .............. Weight ..............

## WAKE UP

## BED TIME

## SLEEP (HRS)

## I'M GRATEFUL FOR

## ACTIVITIES

## EXERCISE LOG

## MOOD TRACKER

- ☐ MORNING
- ☐ AFTERNOON
- ☐ NIGHT

**WATER INTAKE**

## WHAT I ATE TODAY

**BREAKFAST** ..............
**LUNCH** ..............
**DINNER** ..............
**SNACK** ..............

## NOTES

*Happiness Rating* ☆ ☆ ☆ ☆ ☆

# Date _____________ Weight _____________

## WAKE UP

## BED TIME

## SLEEP (HRS)

## I'M GRATEFUL FOR

## ACTIVITIES

## EXERCISE LOG

## MOOD TRACKER

- ☐ MORNING
- ☐ AFTERNOON
- ☐ NIGHT

WATER INTAKE

## WHAT I ATE TODAY

BREAKFAST .............................................................

LUNCH .............................................................

DINNER .............................................................

SNACK .............................................................

## NOTES

Happiness Rating ☆ ☆ ☆ ☆ ☆

# Date _______________ Weight _______________

## WAKE UP

## BED TIME

## SLEEP (HRS)

## I'M GRATEFUL FOR

## ACTIVITIES

## EXERCISE LOG

## MOOD TRACKER

- ☐ MORNING
- ☐ AFTERNOON
- ☐ NIGHT

WATER INTAKE

## WHAT I ATE TODAY

**BREAKFAST** ...........................................................................

**LUNCH** ...........................................................................

**DINNER** ...........................................................................

**SNACK** ...........................................................................

## NOTES

Happiness Rating ★ ★ ★ ★ ★

# Date _______________ Weight _______________

## WAKE UP

## BED TIME

## SLEEP (HRS)

## I'M GRATEFUL FOR

## ACTIVITIES

## EXERCISE LOG

## MOOD TRACKER

- ☐ MORNING
- ☐ AFTERNOON
- ☐ NIGHT

WATER INTAKE

## WHAT I ATE TODAY

**BREAKFAST** ...........................................................................

**LUNCH** ...........................................................................

**DINNER** ...........................................................................

**SNACK** ...........................................................................

## NOTES

Happiness Rating ⭐ ⭐ ⭐ ⭐ ⭐

# Date _______  Weight _______

## WAKE UP

## BED TIME

## SLEEP (HRS)

## I'M GRATEFUL FOR

## ACTIVITIES

## EXERCISE LOG

## MOOD TRACKER

- ☐ MORNING
- ☐ AFTERNOON
- ☐ NIGHT

**WATER INTAKE**

## WHAT I ATE TODAY

**BREAKFAST** ....................................................

**LUNCH** ....................................................

**DINNER** ....................................................

**SNACK** ....................................................

## NOTES

*Happiness Rating* ☆ ☆ ☆ ☆ ☆

# Date _______   Weight _______

## WAKE UP

## BED TIME

## SLEEP (HRS)

## I'M GRATEFUL FOR

## ACTIVITIES

## EXERCISE LOG

## MOOD TRACKER

- ☐ MORNING
- ☐ AFTERNOON
- ☐ NIGHT

**WATER INTAKE**

## WHAT I ATE TODAY

BREAKFAST ..................................................

LUNCH ..................................................

DINNER ..................................................

SNACK ..................................................

## NOTES

*Happiness Rating*  ★ ★ ★ ★ ★

# Date __________  Weight __________

## WAKE UP

## BED TIME

## SLEEP (HRS)

## I'M GRATEFUL FOR

## ACTIVITIES

## EXERCISE LOG

## MOOD TRACKER

- ☐ MORNING
- ☐ AFTERNOON
- ☐ NIGHT

**WATER INTAKE**

## WHAT I ATE TODAY

**BREAKFAST** ....................................................................
**LUNCH** ....................................................................
**DINNER** ....................................................................
**SNACK** ....................................................................

## NOTES

*Happiness Rating* ★ ★ ★ ★ ★

# Date _______ Weight _______

## WAKE UP

## BED TIME

## SLEEP (HRS)

## I'M GRATEFUL FOR

## ACTIVITIES

## EXERCISE LOG

## MOOD TRACKER

- ☐ MORNING
- ☐ AFTERNOON
- ☐ NIGHT

WATER INTAKE

## WHAT I ATE TODAY

BREAKFAST ........................................................................

LUNCH ........................................................................

DINNER ........................................................................

SNACK ........................................................................

## NOTES

Happiness Rating ☆ ☆ ☆ ☆ ☆

# Date _______________ Weight _______________

## WAKE UP

## BED TIME

## SLEEP (HRS)

## I'M GRATEFUL FOR

## ACTIVITIES

## EXERCISE LOG

## MOOD TRACKER

- ☐ MORNING
- ☐ AFTERNOON
- ☐ NIGHT

**WATER INTAKE**

## WHAT I ATE TODAY

**BREAKFAST** ..............................................................

**LUNCH** ..............................................................

**DINNER** ..............................................................

**SNACK** ..............................................................

## NOTES

*Happiness Rating* ★ ★ ★ ★ ★

# Date _______________ Weight _______________

## WAKE UP

## BED TIME

## SLEEP (HRS)

## I'M GRATEFUL FOR

## ACTIVITIES

## EXERCISE LOG

## MOOD TRACKER

- ☐ MORNING
- ☐ AFTERNOON
- ☐ NIGHT

**WATER INTAKE**

## WHAT I ATE TODAY

**BREAKFAST** .................................................................

**LUNCH** .................................................................

**DINNER** .................................................................

**SNACK** .................................................................

## NOTES

*Happiness Rating* ★ ★ ★ ★ ★

# Date _______________    Weight _______________

## WAKE UP

## BED TIME

## SLEEP (HRS)

## I'M GRATEFUL FOR

## ACTIVITIES

## EXERCISE LOG

## MOOD TRACKER

- ☐ MORNING
- ☐ AFTERNOON
- ☐ NIGHT

**WATER INTAKE**

## WHAT I ATE TODAY

**BREAKFAST** ..................................................................................................

**LUNCH** ..................................................................................................

**DINNER** ..................................................................................................

**SNACK** ..................................................................................................

## NOTES

*Happiness Rating*  ☆ ☆ ☆ ☆ ☆

# Date ............ Weight ............

## WAKE UP

## BED TIME

## SLEEP (HRS)

## I'M GRATEFUL FOR

## ACTIVITIES

## EXERCISE LOG

## MOOD TRACKER

- ☐ MORNING
- ☐ AFTERNOON
- ☐ NIGHT

WATER INTAKE

## WHAT I ATE TODAY

BREAKFAST ............................................

LUNCH ............................................

DINNER ............................................

SNACK ............................................

## NOTES

*Happiness Rating* ☆ ☆ ☆ ☆ ☆

## Date .................. Weight ..................

### WAKE UP

### BED TIME

### SLEEP (HRS)

### I'M GRATEFUL FOR

..............................................
..............................................
..............................................
..............................................
..............................................
..............................................
..............................................
..............................................

### ACTIVITIES

### EXERCISE LOG

### MOOD TRACKER

☐ MORNING

☐ AFTERNOON

☐ NIGHT

WATER INTAKE

### WHAT I ATE TODAY

BREAKFAST .............................................
LUNCH .............................................
DINNER .............................................
SNACK .............................................

### NOTES

..............................................
..............................................
..............................................
..............................................
..............................................

Happiness Rating ☆ ☆ ☆ ☆ ☆

# Date ............... Weight ...............

## WAKE UP

## BED TIME

## SLEEP (HRS)

## I'M GRATEFUL FOR

## ACTIVITIES

## EXERCISE LOG

## MOOD TRACKER

☐ MORNING

☐ AFTERNOON

☐ NIGHT

**WATER INTAKE**

## WHAT I ATE TODAY

BREAKFAST ...............

LUNCH ...............

DINNER ...............

SNACK ...............

## NOTES

*Happiness Rating* ★ ★ ★ ★ ★

# Date ............... Weight ...............

## WAKE UP

## BED TIME

## SLEEP (HRS)

## I'M GRATEFUL FOR

....................................................
....................................................
....................................................
....................................................
....................................................
....................................................
....................................................
....................................................

## ACTIVITIES

## EXERCISE LOG

## MOOD TRACKER

☐ MORNING

☐ AFTERNOON

☐ NIGHT

WATER INTAKE

## WHAT I ATE TODAY

**BREAKFAST** ....................................................
**LUNCH** ....................................................
**DINNER** ....................................................
**SNACK** ....................................................

## NOTES

....................................................
....................................................
....................................................
....................................................
....................................................

Happiness Rating ★ ★ ★ ★ ★

# Date .............. Weight ..............

## WAKE UP

## BED TIME

## SLEEP (HRS)

## I'M GRATEFUL FOR

..............................................
..............................................
..............................................
..............................................
..............................................
..............................................
..............................................
..............................................

## ACTIVITIES

## EXERCISE LOG

## MOOD TRACKER

☐ MORNING

☐ AFTERNOON

☐ NIGHT

**WATER INTAKE**

## WHAT I ATE TODAY

**BREAKFAST** ..............................................

**LUNCH** ..............................................

**DINNER** ..............................................

**SNACK** ..............................................

## NOTES

..............................................
..............................................
..............................................
..............................................
..............................................
..............................................

## Happiness Rating ☆ ☆ ☆ ☆ ☆

# Date ............... Weight ...............

## WAKE UP

## BED TIME

## SLEEP (HRS)

## I'M GRATEFUL FOR

...............................................................
...............................................................
...............................................................
...............................................................
...............................................................
...............................................................
...............................................................
...............................................................

## ACTIVITIES

## EXERCISE LOG

## MOOD TRACKER

☐ **MORNING**

☐ **AFTERNOON**

☐ **NIGHT**

**WATER INTAKE**

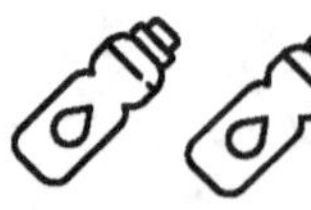      

## WHAT I ATE TODAY

**BREAKFAST** ...............................................................

**LUNCH** ...............................................................

**DINNER** ...............................................................

**SNACK** ...............................................................

## NOTES

...............................................................
...............................................................
...............................................................
...............................................................
...............................................................
...............................................................

*Happiness Rating* ☆ ☆ ☆ ☆ ☆

# Date ______________  Weight ______________

## WAKE UP

## BED TIME

## SLEEP (HRS)

## I'M GRATEFUL FOR

......................................................
......................................................
......................................................
......................................................
......................................................
......................................................
......................................................
......................................................

## ACTIVITIES

## EXERCISE LOG

## MOOD TRACKER

☐ MORNING

☐ AFTERNOON

☐ NIGHT

WATER INTAKE

## WHAT I ATE TODAY

**BREAKFAST** ......................................................

**LUNCH** ......................................................

**DINNER** ......................................................

**SNACK** ......................................................

## NOTES

......................................................
......................................................
......................................................
......................................................
......................................................
......................................................

*Happiness Rating*  ☆ ☆ ☆ ☆ ☆

# Date ............... Weight ...............

## WAKE UP

## BED TIME

## SLEEP (HRS)

## I'M GRATEFUL FOR

## ACTIVITIES

## EXERCISE LOG

## MOOD TRACKER

- ☐ MORNING
- ☐ AFTERNOON
- ☐ NIGHT

WATER INTAKE

## WHAT I ATE TODAY

**BREAKFAST** ...............
**LUNCH** ...............
**DINNER** ...............
**SNACK** ...............

## NOTES

*Happiness Rating* ★ ★ ★ ★ ★

# Date _______  Weight _______

## WAKE UP

## BED TIME

## SLEEP (HRS)

## I'M GRATEFUL FOR

## ACTIVITIES

## EXERCISE LOG

## MOOD TRACKER

☐ MORNING

☐ AFTERNOON

☐ NIGHT

**WATER INTAKE**

## WHAT I ATE TODAY

**BREAKFAST** ......................................................

**LUNCH** ......................................................

**DINNER** ......................................................

**SNACK** ......................................................

## NOTES

*Happiness Rating*  ☆ ☆ ☆ ☆ ☆

# Date _____________  Weight _____________

## WAKE UP

## BED TIME

## SLEEP (HRS)

## I'M GRATEFUL FOR

## ACTIVITIES

## EXERCISE LOG

## MOOD TRACKER

☐ MORNING

☐ AFTERNOON

☐ NIGHT

**WATER INTAKE**

## WHAT I ATE TODAY

BREAKFAST .......................................................................

LUNCH .......................................................................

DINNER .......................................................................

SNACK .......................................................................

## NOTES

Happiness Rating ☆ ☆ ☆ ☆ ☆

# Date _______________ Weight _______________

## WAKE UP

## BED TIME

## SLEEP (HRS)

## I'M GRATEFUL FOR

## ACTIVITIES

## EXERCISE LOG

## MOOD TRACKER

- ☐ MORNING
- ☐ AFTERNOON
- ☐ NIGHT

**WATER INTAKE**

## WHAT I ATE TODAY

**BREAKFAST** ...........................................................................

**LUNCH** ...........................................................................

**DINNER** ...........................................................................

**SNACK** ...........................................................................

## NOTES

*Happiness Rating* ★ ★ ★ ★ ★

# Date _____________ Weight _____________

## WAKE UP

## BED TIME

## SLEEP (HRS)

## I'M GRATEFUL FOR

## ACTIVITIES

## EXERCISE LOG

## MOOD TRACKER

- ☐ MORNING
- ☐ AFTERNOON
- ☐ NIGHT

**WATER INTAKE**

## WHAT I ATE TODAY

**BREAKFAST** ...................................................................................

**LUNCH** ...................................................................................

**DINNER** ...................................................................................

**SNACK** ...................................................................................

## NOTES

Happiness Rating ⭐ ⭐ ⭐ ⭐ ⭐

# Date _____________    Weight _____________

## WAKE UP

## BED TIME

## SLEEP (HRS)

## I'M GRATEFUL FOR

## ACTIVITIES

## EXERCISE LOG

## MOOD TRACKER

- ☐ MORNING
- ☐ AFTERNOON
- ☐ NIGHT

**WATER INTAKE**

## WHAT I ATE TODAY

BREAKFAST .....................................................................

LUNCH .....................................................................

DINNER .....................................................................

SNACK .....................................................................

## NOTES

*Happiness Rating*  ☆ ☆ ☆ ☆ ☆

# Date _______________  Weight _______________

## WAKE UP

## BED TIME

## SLEEP (HRS)

## I'M GRATEFUL FOR

## ACTIVITIES

## EXERCISE LOG

## MOOD TRACKER

- ☐ MORNING
- ☐ AFTERNOON
- ☐ NIGHT

**WATER INTAKE**

## WHAT I ATE TODAY

**BREAKFAST** ...................................................................

**LUNCH** ...................................................................

**DINNER** ...................................................................

**SNACK** ...................................................................

## NOTES

*Happiness Rating* ☆ ☆ ☆ ☆ ☆

# Date ............... Weight ...............

## WAKE UP

## BED TIME

## SLEEP (HRS)

## I'M GRATEFUL FOR

## ACTIVITIES

## EXERCISE LOG

## MOOD TRACKER

- ☐ MORNING
- ☐ AFTERNOON
- ☐ NIGHT

**WATER INTAKE**

## WHAT I ATE TODAY

BREAKFAST ...............................................................

LUNCH ...............................................................

DINNER ...............................................................

SNACK ...............................................................

## NOTES

*Happiness Rating* ★ ★ ★ ★ ★

# Date _______________ Weight _______________

## WAKE UP

## BED TIME

## SLEEP (HRS)

## I'M GRATEFUL FOR

## ACTIVITIES

## EXERCISE LOG

## MOOD TRACKER

- ☐ MORNING
- ☐ AFTERNOON
- ☐ NIGHT

**WATER INTAKE**

## WHAT I ATE TODAY

**BREAKFAST** ..............................................................................................

**LUNCH** ..............................................................................................

**DINNER** ..............................................................................................

**SNACK** ..............................................................................................

## NOTES

*Happiness Rating* ★ ★ ★ ★ ★

# Date ............... Weight ...............

## WAKE UP

## BED TIME

## SLEEP (HRS)

## I'M GRATEFUL FOR

## ACTIVITIES

## EXERCISE LOG

## MOOD TRACKER

- ☐ MORNING
- ☐ AFTERNOON
- ☐ NIGHT

**WATER INTAKE**

## WHAT I ATE TODAY

BREAKFAST ...............

LUNCH ...............

DINNER ...............

SNACK ...............

## NOTES

*Happiness Rating* ☆ ☆ ☆ ☆ ☆

# Date ............... Weight ...............

## WAKE UP

## BED TIME

## SLEEP (HRS)

## I'M GRATEFUL FOR

## ACTIVITIES

## EXERCISE LOG

## MOOD TRACKER

- ☐ MORNING
- ☐ AFTERNOON
- ☐ NIGHT

**WATER INTAKE**

## WHAT I ATE TODAY

**BREAKFAST** ...............................................................

**LUNCH** ...............................................................

**DINNER** ...............................................................

**SNACK** ...............................................................

## NOTES

*Happiness Rating* ☆ ☆ ☆ ☆ ☆

# Date .............. Weight ..............

## WAKE UP

## BED TIME

## SLEEP (HRS)

## I'M GRATEFUL FOR

## ACTIVITIES

## EXERCISE LOG

## MOOD TRACKER

- ☐ MORNING
- ☐ AFTERNOON
- ☐ NIGHT

**WATER INTAKE**

## WHAT I ATE TODAY

BREAKFAST ..............................................................

LUNCH ..............................................................

DINNER ..............................................................

SNACK ..............................................................

## NOTES

# Happiness Rating ★ ★ ★ ★ ★

# Date ........ Weight ........

## WAKE UP

## BED TIME

## SLEEP (HRS)

## I'M GRATEFUL FOR

## ACTIVITIES

## EXERCISE LOG

## MOOD TRACKER

☐ MORNING

☐ AFTERNOON

☐ NIGHT

**WATER INTAKE**

## WHAT I ATE TODAY

**BREAKFAST** ........

**LUNCH** ........

**DINNER** ........

**SNACK** ........

## NOTES

*Happiness Rating* ⭐ ⭐ ⭐ ⭐ ⭐

# Date _____________ Weight _____________

## WAKE UP

## BED TIME

## SLEEP (HRS)

## I'M GRATEFUL FOR

## ACTIVITIES

## EXERCISE LOG

## MOOD TRACKER

- ☐ MORNING
- ☐ AFTERNOON
- ☐ NIGHT

**WATER INTAKE**

## WHAT I ATE TODAY

BREAKFAST _______________________________________

LUNCH _______________________________________

DINNER _______________________________________

SNACK _______________________________________

## NOTES

Happiness Rating  ☆ ☆ ☆ ☆ ☆

# Date _____________ Weight _____________

## WAKE UP

## BED TIME

## SLEEP (HRS)

## I'M GRATEFUL FOR

## ACTIVITIES

## EXERCISE LOG

## MOOD TRACKER

☐ MORNING

☐ AFTERNOON

☐ NIGHT

**WATER INTAKE**

## WHAT I ATE TODAY

BREAKFAST .......................................................

LUNCH .......................................................

DINNER .......................................................

SNACK .......................................................

## NOTES

*Happiness Rating* ★ ★ ★ ★ ★

# Date ............... Weight ...............

## WAKE UP

## BED TIME

## SLEEP (HRS)

## I'M GRATEFUL FOR

.................................................
.................................................
.................................................
.................................................
.................................................
.................................................
.................................................

## ACTIVITIES

## EXERCISE LOG

## MOOD TRACKER

☐ MORNING

☐ AFTERNOON

☐ NIGHT

**WATER INTAKE**

## WHAT I ATE TODAY

BREAKFAST ...............................................

LUNCH ...............................................

DINNER ...............................................

SNACK ...............................................

## NOTES

.................................................
.................................................
.................................................
.................................................
.................................................
.................................................

# Happiness Rating ☆ ☆ ☆ ☆ ☆

# Date ............... Weight ...............

## WAKE UP

## BED TIME

## SLEEP (HRS)

## I'M GRATEFUL FOR

## ACTIVITIES

## EXERCISE LOG

## MOOD TRACKER

- ☐ MORNING
- ☐ AFTERNOON
- ☐ NIGHT

**WATER INTAKE**

## WHAT I ATE TODAY

**BREAKFAST** ...............................................................................

**LUNCH** ...............................................................................

**DINNER** ...............................................................................

**SNACK** ...............................................................................

## NOTES

*Happiness Rating* ★ ★ ★ ★ ★

# Date ................... Weight ...................

## WAKE UP

## BED TIME

## SLEEP (HRS)

## I'M GRATEFUL FOR

## ACTIVITIES

## EXERCISE LOG

## MOOD TRACKER

- ☐ MORNING
- ☐ AFTERNOON
- ☐ NIGHT

**WATER INTAKE**

## WHAT I ATE TODAY

**BREAKFAST** ...................

**LUNCH** ...................

**DINNER** ...................

**SNACK** ...................

## NOTES

*Happiness Rating* ★ ★ ★ ★ ★

# Date _____________ Weight _____________

## WAKE UP

## BED TIME

## SLEEP (HRS)

## I'M GRATEFUL FOR

## ACTIVITIES

## EXERCISE LOG

## MOOD TRACKER

- ☐ MORNING
- ☐ AFTERNOON
- ☐ NIGHT

**WATER INTAKE**

## WHAT I ATE TODAY

**BREAKFAST** .............................................................

**LUNCH** .............................................................

**DINNER** .............................................................

**SNACK** .............................................................

## NOTES

*Happiness Rating* ☆ ☆ ☆ ☆ ☆

# Date ............ Weight ............

## WAKE UP

## BED TIME

## SLEEP (HRS)

## I'M GRATEFUL FOR

## ACTIVITIES

## EXERCISE LOG

## MOOD TRACKER

- ☐ MORNING
- ☐ AFTERNOON
- ☐ NIGHT

**WATER INTAKE**

## WHAT I ATE TODAY

**BREAKFAST** ............

**LUNCH** ............

**DINNER** ............

**SNACK** ............

## NOTES

Happiness Rating ★ ★ ★ ★ ★

Date ................... Weight ...................

## WAKE UP

## BED TIME

## SLEEP (HRS)

## I'M GRATEFUL FOR

## ACTIVITIES

## EXERCISE LOG

## MOOD TRACKER

☐ MORNING

☐ AFTERNOON

☐ NIGHT

WATER INTAKE

## WHAT I ATE TODAY

BREAKFAST .................................................

LUNCH .................................................

DINNER .................................................

SNACK .................................................

## NOTES

Happiness Rating ⭐ ⭐ ⭐ ⭐ ⭐

# Date ............ Weight ............

## WAKE UP

## BED TIME

## SLEEP (HRS)

## I'M GRATEFUL FOR

## ACTIVITIES

## EXERCISE LOG

## MOOD TRACKER

- ☐ MORNING
- ☐ AFTERNOON
- ☐ NIGHT

**WATER INTAKE**

## WHAT I ATE TODAY

**BREAKFAST** ............................................

**LUNCH** ............................................

**DINNER** ............................................

**SNACK** ............................................

## NOTES

*Happiness Rating* ☆ ☆ ☆ ☆ ☆

# Date __________ Weight __________

## WAKE UP

## BED TIME

## SLEEP (HRS)

## I'M GRATEFUL FOR

## ACTIVITIES

## EXERCISE LOG

## MOOD TRACKER

- ☐ MORNING
- ☐ AFTERNOON
- ☐ NIGHT

WATER INTAKE

## WHAT I ATE TODAY

**BREAKFAST** ..................................................
**LUNCH** ..................................................
**DINNER** ..................................................
**SNACK** ..................................................

## NOTES

Happiness Rating ☆ ☆ ☆ ☆

# Date _____________ Weight _____________

## WAKE UP

## BED TIME

## SLEEP (HRS)

## I'M GRATEFUL FOR

## ACTIVITIES

## EXERCISE LOG

## MOOD TRACKER

- ☐ MORNING
- ☐ AFTERNOON
- ☐ NIGHT

WATER INTAKE

## WHAT I ATE TODAY

BREAKFAST .................................................................

LUNCH .................................................................

DINNER .................................................................

SNACK .................................................................

## NOTES

Happiness Rating ⭐ ⭐ ⭐ ⭐

# Date _______________   Weight _______________

## WAKE UP

## BED TIME

## SLEEP (HRS)

## I'M GRATEFUL FOR

## ACTIVITIES

## EXERCISE LOG

## MOOD TRACKER

- ☐ MORNING
- ☐ AFTERNOON
- ☐ NIGHT

**WATER INTAKE**

## WHAT I ATE TODAY

**BREAKFAST** _______________________________________________

**LUNCH** _______________________________________________

**DINNER** _______________________________________________

**SNACK** _______________________________________________

## NOTES

*Happiness Rating* ⭐ ⭐ ⭐ ⭐ ⭐

# Date _______  Weight _______

## WAKE UP

## BED TIME

## SLEEP (HRS)

## I'M GRATEFUL FOR

## ACTIVITIES

## EXERCISE LOG

## MOOD TRACKER

- ☐ MORNING
- ☐ AFTERNOON
- ☐ NIGHT

**WATER INTAKE**

## WHAT I ATE TODAY

**BREAKFAST** ....................................................................

**LUNCH** ....................................................................

**DINNER** ....................................................................

**SNACK** ....................................................................

## NOTES

*Happiness Rating*  ☆ ☆ ☆ ☆ ☆

# Date ............... Weight ...............

## WAKE UP

## BED TIME

## SLEEP (HRS)

## I'M GRATEFUL FOR

## ACTIVITIES

## EXERCISE LOG

## MOOD TRACKER

☐ MORNING

☐ AFTERNOON

☐ NIGHT

**WATER INTAKE**

## WHAT I ATE TODAY

**BREAKFAST** ...............

**LUNCH** ...............

**DINNER** ...............

**SNACK** ...............

## NOTES

*Happiness Rating* ⭐ ⭐ ⭐ ⭐ ⭐

# Date .................... Weight ....................

## WAKE UP

## BED TIME

## SLEEP (HRS)

## I'M GRATEFUL FOR

..........................................................
..........................................................
..........................................................
..........................................................
..........................................................
..........................................................
..........................................................
..........................................................

## ACTIVITIES

## EXERCISE LOG

## MOOD TRACKER

☐ MORNING
☐ AFTERNOON
☐ NIGHT

**WATER INTAKE**

## WHAT I ATE TODAY

BREAKFAST ..........................................................
LUNCH ..........................................................
DINNER ..........................................................
SNACK ..........................................................

## NOTES

..........................................................
..........................................................
..........................................................
..........................................................
..........................................................
..........................................................

*Happiness Rating* ★ ★ ★ ★ ★

# Date _______________ Weight _______________

## WAKE UP

## BED TIME

## SLEEP (HRS)

## I'M GRATEFUL FOR

## ACTIVITIES

## EXERCISE LOG

## MOOD TRACKER

☐ MORNING

☐ AFTERNOON

☐ NIGHT

**WATER INTAKE**

## WHAT I ATE TODAY

**BREAKFAST** .......................................................

**LUNCH** .......................................................

**DINNER** .......................................................

**SNACK** .......................................................

## NOTES

*Happiness Rating* ⭐ ⭐ ⭐ ⭐ ⭐

# Date _______ Weight _______

## WAKE UP

## BED TIME

## SLEEP (HRS)

## I'M GRATEFUL FOR

## ACTIVITIES

## EXERCISE LOG

## MOOD TRACKER

- ☐ MORNING
- ☐ AFTERNOON
- ☐ NIGHT

**WATER INTAKE**

## WHAT I ATE TODAY

**BREAKFAST** .......................................................................

**LUNCH** .......................................................................

**DINNER** .......................................................................

**SNACK** .......................................................................

## NOTES

*Happiness Rating* ⭐ ⭐ ⭐ ⭐ ⭐

# Date ............... Weight ...............

## WAKE UP

## BED TIME

## SLEEP (HRS)

## I'M GRATEFUL FOR

## ACTIVITIES

## EXERCISE LOG

## MOOD TRACKER

☐ MORNING

☐ AFTERNOON

☐ NIGHT

**WATER INTAKE**

## WHAT I ATE TODAY

**BREAKFAST** ...............................................
**LUNCH** ...............................................
**DINNER** ...............................................
**SNACK** ...............................................

## NOTES

*Happiness Rating* ★ ★ ★ ★ ★

# Date _______________ Weight _______________

## WAKE UP

## BED TIME

## SLEEP (HRS)

## I'M GRATEFUL FOR

....................................................

....................................................

....................................................

....................................................

....................................................

....................................................

....................................................

....................................................

## ACTIVITIES

## EXERCISE LOG

## MOOD TRACKER

☐ MORNING

☐ AFTERNOON

☐ NIGHT

WATER INTAKE

## WHAT I ATE TODAY

**BREAKFAST** ....................................................

**LUNCH** ....................................................

**DINNER** ....................................................

**SNACK** ....................................................

## NOTES

....................................................

....................................................

....................................................

....................................................

....................................................

....................................................

*Happiness Rating* ☆ ☆ ☆ ☆ ☆

# Date _____________    Weight _____________

## WAKE UP

## BED TIME

## SLEEP (HRS)

## I'M GRATEFUL FOR

## ACTIVITIES

## EXERCISE LOG

## MOOD TRACKER

- ☐ MORNING
- ☐ AFTERNOON
- ☐ NIGHT

**WATER INTAKE**

## WHAT I ATE TODAY

**BREAKFAST** ...........................................................
**LUNCH** ...........................................................
**DINNER** ...........................................................
**SNACK** ...........................................................

## NOTES

*Happiness Rating*  ★ ★ ★ ★ ★

# Date .............. Weight ..............

## WAKE UP

## BED TIME

## SLEEP (HRS)

## I'M GRATEFUL FOR

## ACTIVITIES

## EXERCISE LOG

## MOOD TRACKER

- ☐ MORNING
- ☐ AFTERNOON
- ☐ NIGHT

WATER INTAKE

## WHAT I ATE TODAY

**BREAKFAST** ..............................................................
**LUNCH** ..............................................................
**DINNER** ..............................................................
**SNACK** ..............................................................

## NOTES

Happiness Rating ☆ ☆ ☆ ☆ ☆

# Date ............ Weight ............

## WAKE UP

## BED TIME

## SLEEP (HRS)

## I'M GRATEFUL FOR

## ACTIVITIES

## EXERCISE LOG

## MOOD TRACKER

- ☐ MORNING
- ☐ AFTERNOON
- ☐ NIGHT

WATER INTAKE

## WHAT I ATE TODAY

**BREAKFAST** ............................................................

**LUNCH** ............................................................

**DINNER** ............................................................

**SNACK** ............................................................

## NOTES

*Happiness Rating* ⭐ ⭐ ⭐ ⭐ ⭐

# Date __________ Weight __________

## WAKE UP

## BED TIME

## SLEEP (HRS)

## I'M GRATEFUL FOR

## ACTIVITIES

## EXERCISE LOG

## MOOD TRACKER

- ☐ MORNING
- ☐ AFTERNOON
- ☐ NIGHT

**WATER INTAKE**

## WHAT I ATE TODAY

BREAKFAST

LUNCH

DINNER

SNACK

## NOTES

Happiness Rating ★ ★ ★ ★ ★

# Date ............... Weight ...............

## WAKE UP

## BED TIME

## SLEEP (HRS)

## I'M GRATEFUL FOR

## ACTIVITIES

## EXERCISE LOG

## MOOD TRACKER

- ☐ MORNING
- ☐ AFTERNOON
- ☐ NIGHT

**WATER INTAKE**

## WHAT I ATE TODAY

**BREAKFAST** ...............
**LUNCH** ...............
**DINNER** ...............
**SNACK** ...............

## NOTES

*Happiness Rating* ★ ★ ★ ★ ★

# Date .................... Weight ....................

## WAKE UP

## BED TIME

## SLEEP (HRS)

## I'M GRATEFUL FOR

.................................................
.................................................
.................................................
.................................................
.................................................
.................................................
.................................................

## ACTIVITIES

## EXERCISE LOG

## MOOD TRACKER

- ☐ MORNING
- ☐ AFTERNOON
- ☐ NIGHT

WATER INTAKE

## WHAT I ATE TODAY

**BREAKFAST** .................................................
**LUNCH** .................................................
**DINNER** .................................................
**SNACK** .................................................

## NOTES

.................................................
.................................................
.................................................
.................................................
.................................................

Happiness Rating ☆ ☆ ☆ ☆ ☆

# Date ................ Weight ................

## WAKE UP

## BED TIME

## SLEEP (HRS)

## I'M GRATEFUL FOR

## ACTIVITIES

## EXERCISE LOG

## MOOD TRACKER

☐ MORNING

☐ AFTERNOON

☐ NIGHT

**WATER INTAKE**

## WHAT I ATE TODAY

**BREAKFAST** ................................................

**LUNCH** ................................................

**DINNER** ................................................

**SNACK** ................................................

## NOTES

*Happiness Rating* ☆ ☆ ☆ ☆ ☆

# Date .................. Weight ..................

## WAKE UP

## BED TIME

## SLEEP (HRS)

## I'M GRATEFUL FOR

## ACTIVITIES

## EXERCISE LOG

## MOOD TRACKER

- ☐ MORNING
- ☐ AFTERNOON
- ☐ NIGHT

**WATER INTAKE**

## WHAT I ATE TODAY

**BREAKFAST** ..................................................

**LUNCH** ..................................................

**DINNER** ..................................................

**SNACK** ..................................................

## NOTES

*Happiness Rating*  ☆ ☆ ☆ ☆ ☆

# Date .................... Weight ....................

## WAKE UP

## BED TIME

## SLEEP (HRS)

## I'M GRATEFUL FOR

## ACTIVITIES

## EXERCISE LOG

## MOOD TRACKER

- ☐ MORNING
- ☐ AFTERNOON
- ☐ NIGHT

**WATER INTAKE**

## WHAT I ATE TODAY

**BREAKFAST** ....................................................

**LUNCH** ....................................................

**DINNER** ....................................................

**SNACK** ....................................................

## NOTES

Happiness Rating ⭐ ⭐ ⭐ ⭐ ⭐

# Date _______________ Weight _______________

## WAKE UP

## BED TIME

## SLEEP (HRS)

## I'M GRATEFUL FOR

## ACTIVITIES

## EXERCISE LOG

## MOOD TRACKER

- ☐ MORNING
- ☐ AFTERNOON
- ☐ NIGHT

WATER INTAKE

## WHAT I ATE TODAY

**BREAKFAST** ........................................................................
**LUNCH** ........................................................................
**DINNER** ........................................................................
**SNACK** ........................................................................

## NOTES

Happiness Rating ⭐ ⭐ ⭐ ⭐ ⭐

# Date _______________  Weight _______________

## WAKE UP

## BED TIME

## SLEEP (HRS)

## I'M GRATEFUL FOR

## ACTIVITIES

## EXERCISE LOG

## MOOD TRACKER

- ☐ MORNING
- ☐ AFTERNOON
- ☐ NIGHT

**WATER INTAKE**

## WHAT I ATE TODAY

BREAKFAST ...............................................................................

LUNCH ...............................................................................

DINNER ...............................................................................

SNACK ...............................................................................

## NOTES

*Happiness Rating* ★ ★ ★ ★ ★

# Date ................ Weight ................

## WAKE UP

## BED TIME

## SLEEP (HRS)

## I'M GRATEFUL FOR

..............................................
..............................................
..............................................
..............................................
..............................................
..............................................
..............................................
..............................................

## ACTIVITIES

## EXERCISE LOG

## MOOD TRACKER

- ☐ MORNING
- ☐ AFTERNOON
- ☐ NIGHT

**WATER INTAKE**

## WHAT I ATE TODAY

BREAKFAST ................................................
LUNCH ................................................
DINNER ................................................
SNACK ................................................

## NOTES

..............................................
..............................................
..............................................
..............................................
..............................................

Happiness Rating ★ ★ ★ ★ ★

# Date ................ Weight ................

## WAKE UP

## BED TIME

## SLEEP (HRS)

## I'M GRATEFUL FOR

## ACTIVITIES

## EXERCISE LOG

## MOOD TRACKER

- ☐ MORNING
- ☐ AFTERNOON
- ☐ NIGHT

**WATER INTAKE**

## WHAT I ATE TODAY

**BREAKFAST** ................................................................

**LUNCH** ................................................................

**DINNER** ................................................................

**SNACK** ................................................................

## NOTES

*Happiness Rating* ⭐ ⭐ ⭐ ⭐ ⭐

# Date ............ Weight ............

## WAKE UP

## BED TIME

## SLEEP (HRS)

## I'M GRATEFUL FOR

## ACTIVITIES

## EXERCISE LOG

## MOOD TRACKER

- ☐ MORNING
- ☐ AFTERNOON
- ☐ NIGHT

WATER INTAKE

## WHAT I ATE TODAY

BREAKFAST ............................................................

LUNCH ............................................................

DINNER ............................................................

SNACK ............................................................

## NOTES

Happiness Rating ⭐ ⭐ ⭐ ⭐ ⭐

# Date _______________  Weight _______________

## WAKE UP

## BED TIME

## SLEEP (HRS)

## I'M GRATEFUL FOR

## ACTIVITIES

## EXERCISE LOG

## MOOD TRACKER

- ☐ MORNING
- ☐ AFTERNOON
- ☐ NIGHT

**WATER INTAKE**

## WHAT I ATE TODAY

**BREAKFAST** ...................................................................................

**LUNCH** ...................................................................................

**DINNER** ...................................................................................

**SNACK** ...................................................................................

## NOTES

Happiness Rating ★ ★ ★ ★ ★

# Date __________ Weight __________

## WAKE UP

## BED TIME

## SLEEP (HRS)

## I'M GRATEFUL FOR

## ACTIVITIES

## EXERCISE LOG

## MOOD TRACKER

☐ MORNING

☐ AFTERNOON

☐ NIGHT

WATER INTAKE

## WHAT I ATE TODAY

BREAKFAST ____________________________________________________

LUNCH ____________________________________________________

DINNER ____________________________________________________

SNACK ____________________________________________________

## NOTES

Happiness Rating ☆ ☆ ☆ ☆ ☆

# Date ............ Weight ............

## WAKE UP

## BED TIME

## SLEEP (HRS)

## I'M GRATEFUL FOR

## ACTIVITIES

## EXERCISE LOG

## MOOD TRACKER

- ☐ MORNING
- ☐ AFTERNOON
- ☐ NIGHT

**WATER INTAKE**

## WHAT I ATE TODAY

**BREAKFAST** ............

**LUNCH** ............

**DINNER** ............

**SNACK** ............

## NOTES

*Happiness Rating* ★ ★ ★ ★ ★

# Date ............ Weight ............

## WAKE UP

## BED TIME

## SLEEP (HRS)

## I'M GRATEFUL FOR

## ACTIVITIES

## EXERCISE LOG

## MOOD TRACKER

☐ MORNING

☐ AFTERNOON

☐ NIGHT

WATER INTAKE

## WHAT I ATE TODAY

**BREAKFAST** ............

**LUNCH** ............

**DINNER** ............

**SNACK** ............

## NOTES

*Happiness Rating* ★ ★ ★ ★ ★

# Date ................ Weight ................

## WAKE UP

## BED TIME

## SLEEP (HRS)

## I'M GRATEFUL FOR

## ACTIVITIES

## EXERCISE LOG

## MOOD TRACKER

- ☐ MORNING
- ☐ AFTERNOON
- ☐ NIGHT

**WATER INTAKE**

## WHAT I ATE TODAY

**BREAKFAST** ................................................

**LUNCH** ................................................

**DINNER** ................................................

**SNACK** ................................................

## NOTES

*Happiness Rating* ★ ★ ★ ★ ★

# Date _______ Weight _______

## WAKE UP

## BED TIME

## SLEEP (HRS)

## I'M GRATEFUL FOR

## ACTIVITIES

## EXERCISE LOG

## MOOD TRACKER

☐ MORNING

☐ AFTERNOON

☐ NIGHT

WATER INTAKE

## WHAT I ATE TODAY

BREAKFAST .......................................................

LUNCH .......................................................

DINNER .......................................................

SNACK .......................................................

## NOTES

Happiness Rating ★ ★ ★ ★ ★

# Date _______________  Weight _______________

## WAKE UP

## BED TIME

## SLEEP (HRS)

## I'M GRATEFUL FOR

## ACTIVITIES

## EXERCISE LOG

## MOOD TRACKER

- ☐ MORNING
- ☐ AFTERNOON
- ☐ NIGHT

**WATER INTAKE**

## WHAT I ATE TODAY

**BREAKFAST** _______________________________________________

**LUNCH** _______________________________________________

**DINNER** _______________________________________________

**SNACK** _______________________________________________

## NOTES

*Happiness Rating*  ☆ ☆ ☆ ☆ ☆

# Date _______ Weight _______

## WAKE UP

## BED TIME

## SLEEP (HRS)

## I'M GRATEFUL FOR

## ACTIVITIES

## EXERCISE LOG

## MOOD TRACKER

- ☐ MORNING
- ☐ AFTERNOON
- ☐ NIGHT

**WATER INTAKE**

## WHAT I ATE TODAY

**BREAKFAST** ....................................................................

**LUNCH** ....................................................................

**DINNER** ....................................................................

**SNACK** ....................................................................

## NOTES

# Happiness Rating ☆ ☆ ☆ ☆ ☆

## Date ............... Weight ...............

### WAKE UP

### BED TIME

### SLEEP (HRS)

### I'M GRATEFUL FOR

### ACTIVITIES

### EXERCISE LOG

### MOOD TRACKER

- ☐ MORNING
- ☐ AFTERNOON
- ☐ NIGHT

**WATER INTAKE**

## WHAT I ATE TODAY

**BREAKFAST** ...............................................................

**LUNCH** ...............................................................

**DINNER** ...............................................................

**SNACK** ...............................................................

## NOTES

*Happiness Rating* ☆ ☆ ☆ ☆ ☆

# Date __________  Weight __________

## WAKE UP

## BED TIME

## SLEEP (HRS)

## I'M GRATEFUL FOR

## ACTIVITIES

## EXERCISE LOG

## MOOD TRACKER

- ☐ MORNING
- ☐ AFTERNOON
- ☐ NIGHT

**WATER INTAKE**

## WHAT I ATE TODAY

BREAKFAST __________________________________

LUNCH __________________________________

DINNER __________________________________

SNACK __________________________________

## NOTES

## Happiness Rating  ☆ ☆ ☆ ☆ ☆

# Date _______________  Weight _______________

## WAKE UP

## BED TIME

## SLEEP (HRS)

## I'M GRATEFUL FOR

## ACTIVITIES

## EXERCISE LOG

## MOOD TRACKER

- ☐ MORNING
- ☐ AFTERNOON
- ☐ NIGHT

**WATER INTAKE**

## WHAT I ATE TODAY

**BREAKFAST** ...............................................................................

**LUNCH** ...............................................................................

**DINNER** ...............................................................................

**SNACK** ...............................................................................

## NOTES

*Happiness Rating*  ★ ★ ★ ★ ★

# Date ............... Weight ...............

## WAKE UP

## BED TIME

## SLEEP (HRS)

## I'M GRATEFUL FOR

....................................................
....................................................
....................................................
....................................................
....................................................
....................................................
....................................................
....................................................

## ACTIVITIES

## EXERCISE LOG

## MOOD TRACKER

- ☐ MORNING
- ☐ AFTERNOON
- ☐ NIGHT

**WATER INTAKE**

## WHAT I ATE TODAY

**BREAKFAST** ....................................................
**LUNCH** ....................................................
**DINNER** ....................................................
**SNACK** ....................................................

## NOTES

....................................................
....................................................
....................................................
....................................................
....................................................
....................................................

**Happiness Rating** ⭐ ⭐ ⭐ ⭐ ⭐

# Date ............... Weight ...............

## WAKE UP

## BED TIME

## SLEEP (HRS)

## I'M GRATEFUL FOR

## ACTIVITIES

## EXERCISE LOG

## MOOD TRACKER

- ☐ MORNING
- ☐ AFTERNOON
- ☐ NIGHT

WATER INTAKE

## WHAT I ATE TODAY

**BREAKFAST** ...............................................................
**LUNCH** ...............................................................
**DINNER** ...............................................................
**SNACK** ...............................................................

## NOTES

Happiness Rating ★ ★ ★ ★ ★

# Date ........................ Weight ........................

## WAKE UP

## BED TIME

## SLEEP (HRS)

## I'M GRATEFUL FOR

........................................................
........................................................
........................................................
........................................................
........................................................
........................................................
........................................................
........................................................

## ACTIVITIES

## EXERCISE LOG

## MOOD TRACKER

- ☐ MORNING
- ☐ AFTERNOON
- ☐ NIGHT

WATER INTAKE

## WHAT I ATE TODAY

BREAKFAST ........................................................
LUNCH ........................................................
DINNER ........................................................
SNACK ........................................................

## NOTES

........................................................
........................................................
........................................................
........................................................
........................................................

Happiness Rating ⭐ ⭐ ⭐ ⭐ ⭐

# Date ................... Weight ...................

## WAKE UP

## BED TIME

## SLEEP (HRS)

## I'M GRATEFUL FOR

## ACTIVITIES

## EXERCISE LOG

## MOOD TRACKER

- ☐ MORNING
- ☐ AFTERNOON
- ☐ NIGHT

**WATER INTAKE**

## WHAT I ATE TODAY

**BREAKFAST** ...................................................................................

**LUNCH** ...................................................................................

**DINNER** ...................................................................................

**SNACK** ...................................................................................

## NOTES

*Happiness Rating* ★ ★ ★ ★ ★

# Date ............ Weight ............

## WAKE UP

## BED TIME

## SLEEP (HRS)

## I'M GRATEFUL FOR

## ACTIVITIES

## EXERCISE LOG

## MOOD TRACKER

☐ MORNING

☐ AFTERNOON

☐ NIGHT

WATER INTAKE

## WHAT I ATE TODAY

BREAKFAST ....................

LUNCH ....................

DINNER ....................

SNACK ....................

## NOTES

Happiness Rating ☆ ☆ ☆ ☆ ☆

# Date _______________  Weight _______________

## WAKE UP

## BED TIME

## SLEEP (HRS)

## I'M GRATEFUL FOR

## ACTIVITIES

## EXERCISE LOG

## MOOD TRACKER

- ☐ MORNING
- ☐ AFTERNOON
- ☐ NIGHT

**WATER INTAKE**

## WHAT I ATE TODAY

**BREAKFAST** .....................................................................................

**LUNCH** .....................................................................................

**DINNER** .....................................................................................

**SNACK** .....................................................................................

## NOTES

*Happiness Rating*  ☆ ☆ ☆ ☆ ☆

# Date _______________  Weight _______________

## WAKE UP

## BED TIME

## SLEEP (HRS)

## I'M GRATEFUL FOR

## ACTIVITIES

## EXERCISE LOG

## MOOD TRACKER

- ☐ MORNING
- ☐ AFTERNOON
- ☐ NIGHT

WATER INTAKE

## WHAT I ATE TODAY

BREAKFAST _______________
LUNCH _______________
DINNER _______________
SNACK _______________

## NOTES

Happiness Rating ★ ★ ★ ★ ★

Date ...................... Weight ......................

## WAKE UP

## BED TIME

## SLEEP (HRS)

## I'M GRATEFUL FOR

..................................................
..................................................
..................................................
..................................................
..................................................
..................................................
..................................................

## ACTIVITIES

## EXERCISE LOG

## MOOD TRACKER

☐ MORNING

☐ AFTERNOON

☐ NIGHT

WATER INTAKE

## WHAT I ATE TODAY

**BREAKFAST** ..................................................
**LUNCH** ..................................................
**DINNER** ..................................................
**SNACK** ..................................................

## NOTES

..................................................
..................................................
..................................................
..................................................
..................................................

Happiness Rating ☆ ☆ ☆ ☆ ☆